1

The Reincarnation of Empress Emma

The events, people and places herein are depicted to the best of the author, who assumes complete responsibility for the accuracy of this narrative.

The American Heritage Dictionary of the English Language, Fifth Edition by the Editors of the American Heritage Dictionaries say reincarnations (noun).

1. A rebirth of mental capacity, such as a soul, in a physical life form, sch as a body.

2. The idea of such a rebirth, a specific belief on how such a rebirth occurs.

3. A fresh embodiment.

4. A new, considerably improved version.

I choose # 4, A new, considerably improved version of myself.

Chapters

1. It is time for me to change

2. My spiritual rebirth

3. My physical rebirth

4. Altar work

5. Mantra's

6. My ancestors calling me

7. Karmas 7 shadows

8. Empress Emma

9. 3rd eye

10. The world is changing

Chapter #1

It's time for me to change

I have been changing spiritually for the past two years. Now it's time for me to change physically. I am overweight. I have survived breast cancer as well as having high blood pressure, high cholesterol and I am a type two diabetic. I have arthritis in both knees which makes it difficult to walk. You really should see me walking up and down the stairs now. In the past I had a cute little walk back in my day. Now my walk consists of me shuffling from side to side with a limp. Not cute at all but at least I can still walk. I'm grateful for that. Just a few years ago I was going to clubs having a few drinks with friends.

Now I spend most of my time in the house. I realized that there is nothing for me out in these streets. I don't really talk to any of my old friends anymore because I'm on a different frequency than they are. I'm also the primary care giver for my three grandchildren while their single mother works. I'm always in the house making sure the two oldest get off to school while baby Chris and I spend our day at home.

I don't really feel good about myself. I feel as though my body is letting me down. I'm so overweight, my hair is greying and thinning on top. I need to see a dentist but since I'm retired, I have to prioritize how I spend my retirement check and dental was low on the list at the time. When I retired, I was living in a nice three-bedroom house with a mortgage, but it was getting more and more difficult to go up and down all those stairs. I knew it was time to downsize because living on a fixed income, there wasn't any extra money to make repairs. It seemed like at that time after living in my house for ten years, everything was starting to fall apart. Every year something needed repair.

I knew I had to declutter my life mentally and physically. It was time for the next chapter in my life. I wanted a smaller place for myself. I kept saying I am going to do something about it, but what? What can I do? I'm not motivated to work out because my knees and legs are in so much pain most of the time. I'm damned if I do and damned if I don't. My doctor wants me to get two knee replacements but I'm not there yet. After I get the kids off to school, I said I was going to try walking around the block with Chris in his stroller. So far that has only happened about two or three times. Either it is too cold to walk or my knees hurt so bad that after the kids get on the school bus, Chris and I just go back in the house.

I have also started doing research on alternative methods on losing weight. That should not be too hard to do because my taste buds are gone. I lost my sense of taste in 2016 when I was diagnosed with breast cancer. Food doesn't taste good any more to me. It seems like the only thing that taste good to me anymore are sweets. I can overdose on those soft peppermints they sell at Walgreens. I am eating some now. I can tell I have put on some weight because my clothes are fitting a little snug right now. I can usually hide my weight in the winter because I can wear more layers of clothing. Summer is around the corner, so I really do need to do something about these extra pounds. Each morning I sit and drink hot water with lemon and a dash of cinnamon to start my day. I read somewhere that drinking lemon water in the morning before you eat any food will curb your appetite for the entire day. We shall see.

Today is the day I have decided to start my work out. My grandchildren and I are going to the Bond Hill Complex where there is an outside area with equipment you can use to strengthen your muscles as well as a walking trail. To the left of the adult area there is a children's play area with swings, slides, and a climbing space. I like to go in the mornings around nine or ten before the sun gets too hot. When we get to the complex the kids run to the play area, Mya takes Chris and put him in the swings. I go to the adult section where I first warm up using the weight machines before I walk the trail. I am glad there are benches around the trail. There is one at the beginning and three more scattered around after that so you can take a break if needed. When I first started, I had to sit down a couple of times before I could finish. I could see the play area from anywhere on the trail and the kids could see me as well. After completing one lap around I would work out for ten minutes on the weights and then do one more lap around the trail. after that I was done. Before I started my work out, I would always say the Miracle Prayer called the Ana B Koach.

The Ana B Koach is the equivalent of the Lord's Prayer. All in all, we would spend about one and a half hours sometimes more because when I was finished the kids wouldn't want to leave. They would be having so much fun.

After sticking to my routine for about two weeks now I can see some results. I have been going to the complex for about two at least three times a week. I can feel the burn when I try to lift my arms. I'm also documenting my workouts by videotaping them. Along with reciting the Miracle Prayer I also acknowledge the Sun God by saying the Sun Mantra. The Blinking Sun Mantra " Let us chant the glories of the Sun God, whose beauty rivals that of a flower. I bow down to him, the greatly effulgent sun of Kasayapa who is the enemy of darkness and destroyer of all sins". You try to get the sun to respond by the sun blinking. It can be done but it takes practice. I haven't been able to do it yet but my son and his wife has.

Tomorrow I have my sixth month check up with my doctor. I haven't been taking any of my medicines my doctor prescribed because I'm trying to live a healthy lifestyle without drugs. I believe the doctors and the Pharmaceutical companies work together. they are the legal drug dealers in my opinion. With all the medicines my doctor prescribes to me, I still have the same illness. They don't cure anything. To help me with my transformation I ordered three books. My first book is The Turmeric Testament. This golden miracle is said to naturally fight pain and inflammation. I love this book because it has over thirty-one recipes for you to try. I also drink the Turmeric Tea every day. The second book is called The Apple Cider Vinegar Miracle. This book has over eighty-one ways to naturally cleans your body and home. The third book is called Inflammation Erased. This book by Susan Patterson is said to naturally fight and reverse damaging inflammatory effects in your body. I've found that in all three books inflammation seems to be the biggest reason for most diseases especially cancer.

As I stated earlier, my doctor doesn't know that I stopped taking the pills he prescribed for me. Now it's time to try something different. I believe the key is to eat healthy, work out and get plenty of rest. I know it's going to take time, but I am determined to stick with it. At least for now. I need to break the cycle of obesity and cancer that runs in my family. Too many of my family members have died from one form of cancer or another. My father died from stomach cancer, my aunt died from ovarian cancer and my mother had breast and lung cancer. I believed my grandmother died from cancer as well.

I have had every illness my mother suffered with. One thing I can be hopeful for is my mother and grandmother lived to be in their eighties.

I believe my survival has been mainly due to my belief in my spiritual journey and the path that I have chosen to take. I will talk more about how my Gods and my spiritual journey have helped me later when I can devote a chapter to that subject. I will talk about how my Gods helped me with my fight against cancer in 2016. I believe everything I have gone through since then have been my subconscious awakening.

Chapter #2

My Spiritual Rebirth

I have been working on my spiritual rebirth for a while now. My son has been practicing his own spiritual beliefs for over seven years now. I can remember him telling me about his altar practices and how he was evolving but I wasn't ready to hear him at that time. I was still partying, hanging out at clubs, drinking, and smoking. When you awaken, your third eye you no longer have the desire to partake in that type of behavior. That all changed when I found out I had breast cancer. I truly believe the more people you have sending up prayers to the heavens the more your prayers are heard and will be answered. I knew I needed help from all the Gods or God to help me make it through this cancer ordeal.

During my rebirth, I now have a better understanding of myself. I now believe there is more to life and death is not the end. Your physical body will die but your spiritual soul will continue on to be reborn again. I love the reincarnation I'm going through. I love talking to my mother, father and all my ancestors that have transitioned on a daily basis. Every morning at 7:00a.m, I start my day by praying to my ancestors at my altar. I say the miracle prayer (The Ana B Koach) three times. I listen to a recording of the mantra (Shreem Brzee) 108 times. Then I give praise and thanks to all my ancestors known and unknown for allowing me to see another day to give praises and thanks to them.

After my altar work is done, I feel refreshed and ready to take on the world. I must say I love talking to my mother and all my ancestors every day. I love saying good morning to them just as if they were all still here with me in this realm. I know their souls are still with me because I can feel them. How else would I have been able to come this far? I try to present myself as the personification of kindness and compassion to everyone I meet. I believe you receive what you put out into the world. I am on this journey that's so high nothing can bring me down.

I find myself staying in the house

more. I don't like being out after dark any more. I don't hang out with any of my old friends anymore because they are not on the same frequency I'm on. You must be around like minded people to evolve. It may seem harsh but sometimes you must distance yourself from family and friends who does not understand your journey. You can't let that stop you because you need to be open and free to receive your blessings so you can unlock your subconscious mind. When you are able to do that you would have opened up all the jewels that have been locked away deep within your third eye vision.

I know I'm in the last trimester of my days here on this earth. That's why I'm preparing my place now for the other realm. I used to be afraid of death but now I know death is just returning from which you came. Returning to that happy place where babies come from right before conception. I have talked to my son (Chris Enlightened) about this and he knows when I transcend to the next life I want to be cremated. I do not want him to spend thousands of dollars to put me in the ground. Keep that money for the living. Take my ashes on a cruise, sprinkle my ashes into the sea where I can join my ancestors who died as slaves journeying here on slave ships from Africa.

Traditionally in my family when someone dies, we have a funeral and burial ceremonies. On some occasions when there isn't any life insurance, the family members will ask for money or put up a go fund me page in order to have enough for the services. I had to do that for my aunt Emma years ago because she had one of those ten cent policies for one thousand dollars that she paid on for twenty years. Boy that insurance company really ripped off our mothers back then. I had to call all the family together and ask for donations to bury her. I got most of the money needed but I still had a balance of one thousand dollars which I made a deal with Garr Funeral Home to make monthly payments until the balance was paid in full.

That's why I just want to be cremated and have a memorial service. I want everyone to remember me in happier times. Have a party for my home going. Let's have a black and white party. My favorite colors. I want a big sheet cake with my picture on it. I can hear Luther singing in the background, "We're having a party". Everyone will be dancing. That is how I want to go out.

Anyway, that's a long way off. While I'm still here I'm continuing my rebirth spiritually and physically. When you are going through your awakening you are always learning and growing. After I started my journey in 2016, after being diagnosed with breast cancer, I wrote about my experiences in my boo (Surviving 2016). At that time in my life I was going about my life without a care in the world and then (Boom) cancer. No one likes to hear you have cancer.

I wasn't new to hearing those words because of my family history but you are still in shock when they are directed at you. when I was diagnosed, it just hit me for a second. I knew I had to do something to overcome this disease. I knew I needed help from the higher power. I immediately turned to my son who had been on his journey for a few years. I called and asked him to pray for me.

It only took two weeks from the time of my diagnosis and my radiation treatment for my torture to be over. Of course, I had regular checkups and additional x-rays to ensure I was cancer free. That's when I became a believer. I joined this spiritual group on Facebook that my son introduced me to. I also constructed my own altar at that time as well as learning new mantras to recite.

The following month I was well enough to attend a spiritual retreat in Gatlinburg Tennessee for four days with my son and his wife. We met twenty other people who themselves were on a spiritual journey as well. We stayed in a very nice cabin that had three floors a jacuzzi, movie theater and plenty of bedrooms along with a full kitchen.

The view was spectacular. Looking out over the treetops because we were high on the mountain top. The road was very winding with no guard rails we felt close to God. We did our morning rituals. We had classes on doing mantras and won prizes playing spiritual games. I especially liked the workshop witch Master Ali Meyers facilitated. In the work shop we learned about our individual talents, abilities, and gifts. My gifts were teaching, healing, and counseling. These are the things I would be good at and most likely to excel at in life. I learned my short-term vision for my gifts are to help people through my books. The Reincarnation of Emma is the fourth book I have published. My first book Ghetto Dreams was written before the retreat and after the retreat I published two more books. This book

I'm writing now is by far my best book because you can actually see my transformation.

On the last day of the retreat our spiritual leader Master Ali Myers posted a you tube segment where we got to speak about our experience on the retreat. I talked about how my life has changed since my subconscious mind has been awakened. I talked about my breast cancer and how I just knew I would be ok due to my new spiritual beliefs. Most of the people there were more advanced than I was. I met Jazz the medium who gave me a reading. She told me one of my ancestors came through who was a heavy-set man walking by me wearing a kangol hat just smiling and laughing. I said, " that's my uncle Louis". I was about ten years old when he transitioned, and I could remember him always laughing and being happy around the family. He had a big belly and when he laughed it shook like a bowl of jelly. She went on to read my son Chris telling him she smelled garlic which was the sign that his Aunt Emma was coming through.

My aunt Emma would always chew on a garlic clove when she was alive. That was some old folk remedy of keeping your heart healthy. It also made her have the worst breath. I was raised by my aunt. When she was alive, she would see ghosts. She would ask me if I saw that man upstairs and I would say no because I wasn't trying to see no ghosts.

My son explained on the you tube video how I healed myself of cancer using my spiritual Gods to remove all obstacles from my body. We both felt it was a miracle how after we prayed the cancer left my body. Of course, the doctors had a hand in it to. Finding out I had cancer was the worst and best day of my life. You might say "how is that the best and worst day of your life"? If I hadn't got cancer I wouldn't have began searching for my spiritual awakening. I would not have been able to open my third eye intuition or my subconscious mind. Once those things are awakened you are on a never-ending journey of seeking knowledge.

People are not aware of this but

when you sleep at night you can astral travel and your ancestors have a better time communicating with you. Most people do not remember any of that when they wake up but if you are in tune with your spiritual side you can astral travel to other realms. I'm not quite there yet but I have heard others talk about how they have been there.

I've been told that sometimes there may be a sacred energy guiding you. If you have been distancing yourself from who and what no longer serves you or lowers your vibration; you've now begun attracting and manifesting who and what serves you. This higher vibration will elevate you, nourish you and inspire you to vibrate higher daily. At this point of discovery, you may find yourself cutting friends and family out of your life. Why you might say? Who wants to be around people who are always complaining, and nothing is going right in their lives? Not me. I don't want negative energy around me. I want to think positive things in my life. How can I evolve higher? What can I do to better myself?. How can I affirm the positivity in my life?

I had this one person in particular who had been my friend for over ten years. I had to cut her out of my life . I haven't talked to her in over two years. I don't answer her phone calls. I haven't been to her house. I missed her last two years birthday parties. All because she is not on the same spiritual path as I 'm on. The main reason is she disrespected me two years ago in a negative way and after that I decided I didn't need that in my life anymore.

I'm sixty-four years old. The time is now to start preparing for the next chapter in my life. I pray to my ancestors for guidance. I ask Lord Ganesha to protect and remove all obstacles from my life. I'm getting ready for the next realm. I can feel it coming. My whole attitude about life is changing.

There was this one night a few months ago where I was sleeping. I could feel myself being drawn to this bright light. I felt as though I was floating towards this light, but I didn't want to go to the light. Just as I felt my self being pulled closer and closer to the light. I was thinking this is the end. The next thing I remember I was falling out of my bed. Now I can't remember the last time I fell out of bed. As I lay there for a while afraid of going to another realm and I didn't know what was happening at that time. I forced myself to wake up. Or maybe the entity on the other side knew I was not ready yet. Either way I feel myself getting more and more Intune with my rebirth or my reincarnation.

Chapter #3

My Physical Rebirth

I am now trying to change my physical body. I'm getting more sun which is vitamin D. Hello to the Sun God Kasayapa who is the enemy of darkness and destroyer of all sins. We all need more vitamin D in our lives. I try to get at least ten minutes of sun rays every morning by saying the blinking sun mantra. Let us chant the glories of the Sun God whose beauty rivals that of a flower. I bow down to him the greatly effulgent Sun God. I have also started to change my eating habits. I'm drinking more water than I have before. I quit drinking sodas and started drinking more teas.

I've started drinking this detox tea every morning. It consists of Turmeric Tea with a slice of lemon and a pinch of cinnamon and honey for sweetness. I'll also have a boiled egg and a slice of wheat toast. Later that day for a pick me up I might have a banana smoothie with a scoop of skinny fit powder enriched with multi collagen with peptides. The skinny fit powder is to help promote healthy bones and joints. At least that's what they claim. I will try this product for six months. If it works, I will document the results.

I've also been limiting my meat intake. I'm eating more fruits and vegetables. I used to love when my Aunt made salmon cakes. I could never make them like she did. Mama Vivian makes some mean ones now. I go over to her house every Sunday to taste her famous cooking. I found a recipe and tried my hand at cooking some. My granddaughter loved them so much she ate three.

To suppress my appetite, I will drink this in the morning before I eat anything. You need a tablespoon of raw honey, teaspoon of cinnamon powder and 1/2 lemon squeezed. Mix all in a cup of warm water. Drink once a day on an empty stomach. I like using these ingredients because they are good for weight loss. I love to use cinnamon because it is good for inflammation. Inflammatory fighting foods are good for fighting water retention and can also help to prevent heart and kidney problem which all I have. Using cinnamon and lemon together in a water drink can help regulate your blood sugar level.

I found this and other recipes like this in Susan Patterson's book (Inflammation Erased). I have type 2 diabetes. In Susans book it states," Treating diabetes with drugs may pose a wide variety of dangers". She also states" utilizing drugs to treat type 2 diabetes may be quite harmful, and some research has found that these drugs my actually kill you". My doctor prescribed two high pressure medications, cholesterol, and diabetic pills for me. One prescription was Lisinopril 10 MG tablets. Let me tell you. This pill I took for about three months. All of a sudden, I started to have this scratching in my throat and really bad cough. I didn't know what was wrong with me. All night long I would be coughing and sneezing. Then I googled the side effects of it and that's what it was. As soon as I stopped taking it, I stopped coughing. Another one of my medicines I couldn't take because I have a problem swallowing big pills was for my diabetes. So now I take Trulicity which is one shot a week I give myself in my leg. So far so good with the shots. Some medicines side effects could cause amputation of toes, feet and legs. My cousin Mary just recently had to have one of her big toes amputated. So you can see why I feel like I'm damned if I do and damned if I don't. I just keep praying it will all work out for me.

There is another recipe that I haven't tried yet called the morning shot. You take four cups water, 1/4 cup raw honey, 1/4 cup ACV, 1 tsp turmeric powder and 1/8 tsp cayenne pepper. Heat over medium heat. Pour into pitcher, refrigerate overnight. In the morning pour in shot glass and drink. I haven't tried that yet but I have started taking this stuff called Sea Moss which I put in my tea. you can use it in smoothies, soups and desserts. I put it in my tea at night. It is supposed to help with sustained energy and healthy skin and hair. All things I'm lacking in.

I have a history of a lot of overweight people in my family. The Colbert Family was known for being big people. Throughout the years I have watched some of them die from heart failure, obesity and other related illnesses. I'm trying to end this generational problem by re-inventing myself. I would love to be able to dance again after I remove all of this weight from my body. The only thing that has been slowing me down are my knees. Some days they hurt so bad I have to stay in bed. Years ago when I was still working my knees would just give out on me and I had to stay in bed a few days until I could walk again. My doctor wants me to have a double knee replacement, but I don't like surgery. If it's not life or death I'm not having it. I know I'm a big baby. I've just gotten use to the pain. I've had the usual cortisone shots in my knees. Nothing works forever.

I'm trying everything that I think can help. I just started taking CBD oil as well as this new Olive Leaf Extract. Hopefully, it will help. The Olive Leaf is said to help lower blood pressure, diabetic blood sugar, parasites, eczema, lupus, candida yeast and increase restful sleep. Wow! That's a lot. All in all I'm hopeful about my outcome.

Chapter #4

Altar Work

I have stated in the previous chapters that I start every day at 7:00a.m. with prayers at my altar. Doing my altar work should be just like breathing. It's something I need to do every day. Since 2016, when I first began my awakening, I have spent ten to twenty minutes every morning praying to my ancestors and Gods thanking them for allowing me to see another day, to learn and grow spiritually.

My son Chris Enlightened helped

me start my first altar. If you go on You Tube and search for Thee Enlightened Journey, you can find all of his videos on how to begin and ancestor or deity altar. In chapter #1 I started to talk about my spiritual journey and how it's helps me.

Some people may say aren't you lonely staying in the house all the time. My reply would be no. I have all my ancestors with me. I am now in tune with my inner self. Even growing up as a child I would feel better being in the house by myself. I would think and imagine how I would want my life to be.

I always felt alone like I wasn't loved, or I wasn't good enough.

I believe that's why I left home as early as I did. I got married at seventeen years old. I wanted to start a family as soon as possible so I could have someone to love me. Of course, that was a disaster. I married my childhood sweetheart. A year later I had my son Chris. I still wasn't happy because my then husband tried to control me just like my Aunt had done. It was like jumping out of the frying pan into the fire. I talked about that situation in my first book "Ghetto Dreams".

Back to altar work. You need to have four elements to start your altar. They are Earth, Wind, Fire and Water. You will need a small wooden table to set up preferably one the east wall of the room. Place a cloth over the table. For the Earth element you can use either crystals or a plant. For the Wind element you should use incense. For the Fire element you use a candle. For the Water element you can use either a bowl or bottle of water. Other items you may place on your altar are things your ancestors enjoyed. Say for instance your ancestor loved smoking, you could place a cigarette for them on the altar. If your aunt like candy you could place a piece of candy for them on your altar. Other items I place on my altar are pictures of my ancestors like their obituary after they are no longer on this physical earth.

My aunt Emma, who raised me, loved to drink old Taylor whiskey so I would place a shot of old Taylor on the altar. Now it's time to start your altar work. First, I light my candles which is like a doorway for the spiritual world. I have a singing bowl that I would hit three times like a doorbell to let my ancestors know I'm at my altar. Next, I would burn ancestor money. You can order ancestor money from any metaphysical shop online. The reason you burn ancestor money is because your ancestor still owes a debt here in the physical world and when we burn money in this realm they can use the money for anything they might need in their realm. While burning the money you say, " this is for all my ancestors known and unknown".

Now we are ready to start praying. I really like you tube because you can literally find anything you need there. I like the spiritual mantras you can find there. While I'm praying, I like to listen to the recording of the Lord Ganesha Mantra called shreem brzee playing in the background. It's something about how the Monks say the prayers that get me in the mood to meditate. This mantra is repeated one hundred eight times.

I say "to all my ancestors known and unknown please know in my heart that I love you". "Thank you for waking me up this morning and protecting me and my family while we were sleeping"." Forgive me of any negativity I have had in the past or future". "Thank you for placing me on the right path to learn and to grow on my spiritual journey".

Another prayer I say every morning is " we give thanks to our creator for allowing me to overcome my humanity in this place we claim our divinity and look to God for guidance. We your children accept our light and divinity in this place. On this day we rise. On this day we give thanks for the gifts of power you have placed in our lives". After that prayer I will say my favorite Mantras. One is Om Gum Ganapatayei Namaha. The translation means; I bow down to the elephant -faced deity (Ganesha) who is capable of removing all obstacles. I pray for blessings and protection. Lord Ganesha is the God of wisdom, success and the destroyer of all obstacles.

Before I began my journey and knew about Lord Ganesha I was in love with collecting elephants. I had an elephant collection of pictures, hanging masks, earrings, and bracelets. Anything having to do with elephants I had to have it. I now realize that was my subconscious mind calling me to Lord Ganesha. I didn't quite know why I loved elephants so much then but now I know. After you've done all your praying and saying your mantras it's now time to give your offerings to your ancestors. Ancestor food is very important You don't have to go overboard. Just give a small portion of whatever you eat and place it on your altar. As you can see taking care of your altar is like taking care of a baby. You give offerings out of love. When you give to your ancestors, they in turn give back to you. All you have to do is ask for what you want. After asking for what you want don't forget to say "thank you, thank you, thank you, three times".

Ok, now that you know how to set up your altar; remember your altar is like a living entity. Your altar should always keep growing with your spiritual awakening. My first altar was on a small wooden table but now my altar almost takes up my whole living room. I now have my crystals, statue of Buddha and Lord Ganesha on my altar. I have a room full of plants surrounding my altar which makes my altar feel alive to me. I also love to burn sage at my altar. The visual of my plants makes me feel as though I'm out in the forest meditating with the aroma of sage cleansing my soul. Burning sage is very good for clearing out bad karma or evil spirits from your home.

When I first moved into my apartment, after down sizing from my house, I blessed my apartment by going room to room carrying my sage asking the Gods to remove all negative forces from my home. When you enter my home, I have a cross that belonged to my Aunt hanging on the wall and a small statue of Lord Ganesha above my door frame so no evil will enter into my home.

That's why I believe I love being in my home. There is just so much evil out in the streets. I feel safe and loved surrounded by all my ancestors. I talk to my mom every day at my altar. I say good morning mom and all my other relatives that's gone on. I also say my Ana B Koach miracle prayer in the

morning or anytime during the day when the feeling comes over me to do so. The Ana B Koach miracle prayer is the equivalent of the Lord's prayer to Catholics.

If someone is sick you can say the Ana B Koach prayer to help heal them. This past summer my last surviving aunt, Aunt Sister, was in the hospital on her death bed. She looked like she was ready to go on. She couldn't talk. She couldn't open her eyes. My cousins

Laura and her Mother came up from Tennessee to pay their respects to her. While we were all in the hospital, we started to recite the Ana B Koach prayer and then our aunt opened up her eyes and smiled. This is a fact. I saw with my own eyes. I truly believe she heard our prayers and they were answered. My aunt came around and was able to go home. She did however pass on two months later at her own home surrounded by people who loved her.

I have a few other prayers written down that I say every day but you must memorize The Ana B Koach prayer for it to be effective. I was also challenged to memorize another prayer called the body of light mantra. You would use the body of light mantra to give praise to the sun God. You should say this prayer at sunrise every morning, but you can recite it whenever the feeling moves you as well.

Chapter# 5

Mantras

My daughter finally convinced me to move in with her and her child's father. I have been on my own since I was seventeen and I had to think really hard about this move. I said ok because I had her children most of the time while she worked. She was always working long hours and it seemed like she never saw the kids. If I moved in with her she could have more time raising her own children.

The initial move in was smooth

because I put most of my things in storage and everything else, I got rid of. All of my furniture got thrown away because when we move into the new house, we want everything new. The plan is to live in the apartment for two years then move into a bigger house.

I feel the rolls are reversed. I'm living in my daughter's home and I'm not going to pay any rent. They need to pay me. I'm the nanny, cook and chauffeur. I drive the kids to and from school. I clean the house. But I don't mind. This is my life now. That's what grandparents do. I really don't do that much because Chris father is Mr. Mom. He does most of the cooking. He helps Mya and Tony with their homework. He even brought me dinner in bed. I said "wow" he's a keeper.

The only thing I really miss about my apartment is I had more room to set up my altar. Now I have a small table in the corner where I store all my altar items in a box under the table. Each morning I remove everything from the box set up my altar, say my prayers and put back everything in the box under the table.

Since I'm at the midway point of my reincarnation I'm going to take time to do research on my spirituality. I found this site that will do a person's numerology report. A numerology report will tell what kind of person you are and who you really are. Your numerology is determined by the letters in your full name at birth and the date and time you were born. Numerology is like a little guide that will awaken your sixth sense or your third eye.

I would also like to talk about your

Guardian Angels. The day we were born we all had a special Angel looking after us. Your Guardian Angel walks side by side with you every day. I can remember looking back over my life there were times where I could have died or been seriously hurt, and I would say boy I was lucky. No, my Angel was looking after me. After doing my research I found out my Guardian Angels name is Uriel. Uriel is known as the " Angel of Light". Uriel is the truth bringer in this world and shines a light during our darkest times, Uriel is the angel to call upon when all seems lost. I also like the Archangel

Barakiel. I call upon the Archangel Barakiel to serve me and raise my power of light and bring me into greater gold and light. My Archangel says I'm a peacemaker. That's true because I'm always the one who tries to keep the peace in any situation. Little children seem to always gravitate towards me too. I have a strong intuition, and my greatest strength is my spirituality. I have always had the sense of doing good and telling the truth. I just cannot tell a lie.

I usually can read people instantly. I

can tell if I'm going to like you or not. One of the things I like to work on during my reincarnation is my ability to see the positive and negative equally in all things. I tend to hone in on the negative too much. By thinking negatively, you can bring it to life. I now try to always see the positive and good in things. I know I need to discover my life's purpose. What was I put here on this earth to do? I used to think it was to raise a well-rounded family. Break the generational curse of my family. I always thought of myself as the black sheep of the family. Why was I not raised with my biological mother or father? Why did my two sisters take on the light skin complexion of our mother and I took on my father's darker complexion? Why in all my relationship I was the one who chose to leave the relationship?

I finally realized that we only spend time with people for a season and a reason. We may not always know the reason, but we know when it feels right to stay or leave. I believe we all have psychic abilities living dormant in our minds. It's up to you to bring these abilities out in the open. Some people in their dream state can bring to life situation from their dream state into reality. Have you ever had a dream about something, and it actually came true? I know I might never get all the answers to my questions, but I have become accepting to the life I have. I learned to love myself first. I realized all of this through meditation and my rebirth.

Spending a lot of time with my grandchildren has brought me back in time. I can remember when my children were young and how I dealt with them. I can see the same characteristics in my grandchildren that I saw in their mother when she was their age. I know some grandmothers can't be bothered with their grandchildren, but I love mines to death. I've always been a nurturer. Rather it's with people or plants. I like to plant seeds and watch them blossom.

To keep me in tune with my Deities , Gods and Guardian angels I like to say Mantras. Mantras are words or affirmations you use to motivate you through meditations. Repeating mantras over and over again will inspire you to be your best self. My son has a mantra he uses all the time. Whenever you ask him how he's doing he says "Winning". A mantra can be anything you try to invoke within you. It should always be something positive such as "I choose to be a better version of me" or "I am all that I can be now".

I have several mantras that I use when I'm meditating. I use the Om mantra. Most mantras should be repeated one hundred eight times. This technique is called chanting. You can either chant out loud , whisper or repeat in your mind. Other mantras I say daily are "om Gum Ganapataye Namaha" which means I bow to elephant-faced deity Ganesha who is capable of removing all obstacles. I will probably say this mantra several times throughout this book because Lord Ganesha is the deity I most relate to. Lord Ganesha is like my heavenly Father. Other than my guardian Angel he is who I call on in times of need. Another mantra I use a lot is Shreem Brzee which is used to ask for wealth. You say this mantra over and over to invoke it's power with in your subconscious mind to achieve wealth. I'm not a wealthy person but there have been times where I needed money for a bill or to buy food and I chanted that morning and out of nowhere I got the money I needed. I can't tell you why some people are wealthy, and others are not. I do believe we all have been here before. Many times. Maybe in those other lives you were wealthy and in this life you are not so you can grow and see what you need to work on.

Chapter #6

Ancestors Calling Me

I can feel my ancestors calling me. I pray to them every day at my altar. I've had dreams where I have felt my ancestors pulling me towards them. You have to be open to it though. If your subconscious mind is not awakening, your soul will not be able to advance to the next level. In a way we are stuck to one reality here on earth unless you have unlocked the code to the next realm. I've only been on my spiritual journey since 2016.

I have always been religious and spiritual all my life but it hasn't been until now that my third eye have been awakened and I am now aware of all my ancestors and deities that are protecting me. Have you ever experienced de ja vu? What about karma? These experiences may have something to do with your past experiences in the past or another life time. Sometime there is a generation of karma in your family.

Has someone ever told you that you look just like your deceased grandfather or another family member?

You may have a generation of alcoholics in your family. My father had over twenty-five children with six different women. There's no way he could have spent quality time with all those children. That song by the Temptations "Papa was a rolling stone, wherever he laid his hat was his home and when he died all he left us was alone". We used to laugh and say, "that's our father".

My father was a tall, dark skin, handsome man. He was a slow walking, smooth talking man who was never in a hurry to get anywhere. I was raised by his sister, my name sake, Aunt Emma. My Aunt would always take me around his other children by those other women because she said" you need to know who your brothers and sisters are" so when you grow up you want be dating your family and not know who they are.

I think about my family members all the time who have crossed over to the other realm. I have some of their pictures on my ancestor altar. I say good morning to my mother, father and uncles and all my ancestors known and unknown every morning. I never had a problem with my father not being in my life. I just excepted him for who he was. Although my biological mother didn't raise me, I knew her and visited her and my siblings every weekend when I was younger. So, my mother was in my life. I remember when I was about six or seven years old my aunt Emma would put me on a bus, tell the driver what street to let me off on and my older sister would be waiting for me at the bus stop. That's how I would get to my mother's house to visit. You couldn't do that in today's times.

Recently I had a reading where a psychic told me that a man came through touching his stomach, holding his head saying he was sorry for not being in my life. I knew she was talking about my father. My father died from stomach cancer, but I never really had a problem with him not being in my life. I just excepted him for who he was. I reconciled with him on that. He even walked me down the aisle at my wedding.

When you are born you choose your parents. I know I chose my parents for a reason. My mother was this loving, forgiving, caring person and my father was just my father. Both of my parents taught me very important lessons. By my father essentially abandoning me and all his children, It helped me deal with other abandonment issues later in life with my husband and other men in my life doing the same thing.

Now my mother on the other hand was the sweetest most loving person I had ever known. The story I was told about how my aunt came to raise me was; my mother after she gave birth to me was really sick and had to go to the hospital. My aunt Emma volunteered to take care of me while my mon was in the hospital. After my mom came home, she did try to get me back but my aunt kept saying " let me keep her for one more week". One more week became another week and another week until my aunt just kept me. My aunt could not have any children of her own, so she was very persistent about keeping her name sake. After all my mother had five other children at home at that time.

I know I have both combine traits

from my mother and father. My zodiac sign is Scorpio and my numerology soul urge is eleven. A soul urge of eleven means It speaks of things I yearn for the most. What motivates me and my true intentions. Why I do the things I do. Put all that together. My father was a lover and my mother was a nurturer and care giver. I can relate to both traits. My chosen field for my thirty-two-year career was security. To serve and to protect. After my retirement I was the care giver for my three young grandchildren. I could see myself following in my mother's footsteps.

Always putting my family first and foremost before all others.

My friends would always say" you spend too much time watching your grandchildren". You need a life too. I would tell them " my family is my life". I love my grandchildren and I want my grandchildren to remember me as a loving grandma.

Nurturer: Definition Word origin- to feed and to protect; to nurture one's offspring. To support and encourage, as to bring up; train; educate. I have always felt like a nurturer. I love my entire family and I would do anything for them. I feel the same way about my ancestors. I can feel them around me always watching over me. I want them to be proud of me and how I have raised my family. I'm so proud of my number one son Chris Enlighten. My first born. Even as a baby I knew he was going to be a light on this world. I watched him grow into this amazing young man and now as an adult he has surpassed all my expectations of him. He is the ambassador for all our family and our ancestors. He ensures all of our ancestors are taken care of. That's why when I leave this realm, I know I will be taken care of as well. My son is the reason why I have also found my spiritual path. I reached out to him when I found out I had breast cancer and he showed me how to reach out to my ancestors, guardian angels and the deities I connect to. More and more each day I feel the connection to the other realm.

My second born Teenya. She had a rough time starting out as a child. She had a hard time learning in school.

Doctors wanted to put her on Ritalin a Methylphenidate which is a stimulant used to treat ADHD. The doctors kept labeling her with Attention-deficit. I did try that with her for about two months, but the side effects left her looking like a zombie. she was moving in slow motion and my aunt Emma said to me, "If you don't take her off that damn drug". And I did because I could see the change in her.

A few years later there was an event at my job and there was a psychic there. I asked would my daughter be ok in life. The psychic name was Mary Lou. What a coincident I had an aunt named Mary Lou. She told me Teenya would be ok.

Even though my daughter did have a few devastating occurrences with having two stillbirth babies when she first attempted to have children. We overcame that tragedy and she now has three beautiful children and a great career. So all in all I have two great children that I know My ancestors are looking down and smiling on all of us. My ancestors are watching over me.

Chapter #7

Karma's 7 Shadows

My son once told me that children choose their parents. I chose my mother and father. You chose your mother and father. Why? To learn from them. Before we were born, our souls connected with our birth parents' souls. It doesn't matter if you had a perfect parent or a drug addicted crack addict parent. We choose our parents to learn and grow so we can cut the karmic pain and generational curse of your ancestors.

There are seven karmic shadows in every family:

1. Abuse

2. Addiction

3. Violence

4. Poverty

5. Illness

6. Abandonment

7. Betrayal

Your family may have one or all seven shadows in your family tree. As I look back on my family tree I can truly say that I have witnessed all seven shadows in my lifetime.

The first shadow I experienced was abandonment. I was given to my aunt by my mother to raise as her own. My aunt couldn't have any children of her own.

As I stated before my mother already named me after my aunt Emma. As I was told when I was six months old my mother needed to go to the hospital for a few days. My aunt volunteered to watch ne until she came home. As I was told every time my mother came back to get me my aunt would persuade her to let her keep me for just one more week. One week became two more weeks until my aunt just kept me.

My aunt told my mother she could do more for me because my mother already had five children at home that she was taking care of. Almost like my aunt could give me a better life.

The next shadow I experienced was poverty. In the fifties, most black people lived in poverty. We lived in the projects or low-income housings my entire childhood. My mom lived in the Winton terrace housing and my aunt and I lived in the Lincoln court housing.

My aunt was working as a bar maid at the Black Beer Lot before she got me. She wanted a more respectable job and the only other job she could get with little education was working as maid for white people. She did take good care of me in her own way. I always got whatever I wanted, and she worked hard to provide for me. If I got dirty, she would change my clothes sometimes as much as three times because she wanted me to be this perfect little child.

The next shadow was abuse. My

aunt ruled with an iron hand. She was extremely strict. My earliest remembrance of abuse was at the age of five years old. I can't remember why I was getting disciplined, but I do remember taking off all my clothes lying across a stool while my aunt placed her leg around my neck. She would then beat me on my exposed bottom. I could not move at all. I don't remember to much after that age. I read somewhere that if you experience trauma you may block years out of your life. What could I have done? My next memories were in my teen years. I think I must have astral traveled out of my body to escape the abuse I suffered.

At the age of fourteen I remember going over my cousins house to play. My cousins wanted me to spend the night so we decided to walk back to my house to ask my aunt if I could spend the night. I knew I was supposed to be home before the streetlights came on. My cousins were playing taking their time to get to my house. It was getting darker and darker by the time we reached my house. The streetlights were on at this time. I was so scared, so I told my sister

Sharon and my cousin Vanessa to go in before me. I told everyone else to wait outside. When I walked in all I remember was my aunts hands grabbing me around my neck then throwing me down on the bed in the bed room. She began to beat me with a Louisville slugger miniature baseball bat.

When she was done, she told my sister and cousin who were in the living room to leave because I wasn't going anywhere. I felt so embarrassed because I knew everyone downstairs herd my screams. To make matters worse after she beat me, she instructed me to do some ironing for extra punishment. When I tried to pick up the iron I couldn't. It was like my hand was sprung from the repeated beating it received while I was trying to protect my butt from the repeated blows she was giving it. When I told her, I couldn't use my hand she told me to use the other hand.

After she said that to me it was like something just came over me and I said " I want to go back to my real mother". I felt anything was better than living with mommy dearest.

At this time, my mother was living in Avondale with seven children and I made eight. My aunt took me back to my mom and she said she would give me bus fare to go back and forth to school. My aunt would come by the house while I was at school to talk to my mother. She would tell my mother that I could come back home anytime I wanted to, but my mother wasn't supposed to tell me this.

This went on about two weeks. My aunt came by with a brand-new car to show me. She said I could drive it if I came back home. I knew she was trying to bribe me. I gave in and went back.

My aunt was also keeping my little cousin Laura because her mom was in a bad way. Laura was about three or four years old at that time. I was in for a shock when I walked into that house. I saw little Laura sitting on the couch. She had two black eyes and a huge knot on her forehead. I asked, " what happened to Laura". My aunt said, "she fell off the couch". Now our couch was very low to the floor so she would have had to jump up in the air, do a flip, dive on the floor to get injuries like that.

At that point in time I knew I had made the right choice to return home if just to protect Laura. I also knew that my aunt would not beat me anymore because she knew I would leave if she ever did again.

Addiction: Laura's mother was addicted to heroin I believe. After her last son was born with birth defects, she started to get clean. I remember I was sixteen and I would drive her to a Clifton center to get her methadone treatments. My aunt Emma was an alcoholic. There were times after she had gone out, she would not remember where she parked the car or the car would be parked so crooked in the parking spot.

I can remember as early as ten driving my aunt home after we had visited a friend houses because she was too drunk to drive. I would be so scared. I asked, "what if the police pull me over" she said "just tell them I'm drunk". That's my aunts mentality. Other times when she and her friends were drinking in the car she would take me to the Union Terminal so I could practice driving around and around while they partied. That's how I learned to drive very well.

Violence; was no stranger to me. I used to see my aunt and her sister aunt Mary Lou fight all the time. One time while I was driving them around my aunt Mary Lou started grabbing and beating my aunt Emma in the car. Why? I don't know but my aunt Emma would not hit my aunt Mary Lou back. Now my aunt Mary Lou was a fighter. She once threw lye in the face of one of her boyfriends. Another time she set fire to her hallway in order to burn up another boyfriend sleeping in her bed.

I couldn't wait to graduate high school get married in order to leave my house. I graduated high school at seventeen. I married my childhood sweetheart at eighteen and had my first-born son at nineteen. Soon after that my husband started down a spiral path of losing job after job after job. That's when the physical altercations started. We would fight all the time. I jumped out of the fire into the frying pan leaving my mother's house then marring my husband.

I tried to make it work. I told my husband that if he couldn't keep a job, he needed to join the military. I had a good job at the federal reserve bank I got right out of high school. After my husband finished boot camp it was time for me to make a decision. Being a good wife, I quit my job, moved to Jacksonville with my family. Before we left my aunt told me if it doesn't work out to call her and she would send me bus fare.

The same thing happened in

Florida. We fought all the time. If I asked him for a dollar, he would give me fifty cents. I was used to having my own money. I didn't know anyone in Florida. I was gaining weight because all I did was sit home take care of our son and eat. That only lasted one year because that's what I told my husband how long I would give us there. So, after one year my aunt sent the money and I packed up my son and moved back to Cincinnati.

My aunt knew that wasn't going to work. I didn't like that Gilbert would bring his navy friends home. They would be drinking and smoking in the house. Gilbert would put beer in his sons bottle at two years old. The phrase cuss like a sailor is true. My baby could barely talk but he was cussing like his father. That's another reason I wanted to leave. I did not want my son to grow up like that.

Illness: my family has had a lot of cancer in our history. Both of my grandparents died from cancer. My aunt Emma and my father and mother both had cancer. I myself was a cancer survivor. There has been mental illness in my family. I had an uncle who committed suicide by jumping out a third-floor window when I was about eight years old.

I bet if I go back into my family history, I can find other ancestors who have died from the same type of illnesses. Every family has a history of the seven shadows of karma in their family. The cancer gene seems to be the most noticeable shadow over my family. When in 2016 I myself found out I had breast cancer it wasn't a shock to me. That's also the time when I started my spiritual journey. I was calling on my ancestors and they healed me.

So in a way, getting cancer was a good thing because getting cancer started me on the path of spiritual healing, opening up my third eye and being in tune with my ancestors and Gods.

Chapter #8

Empress Emma

Empress meaning; Love, Health and Money. Feminine power-fertility, abundance nurture, and love of home and family. I can feel myself changing. I have always been kind of a loner but now I pray every day to my ancestors, and I don't feel alone anymore.

The whole world is changing. it's now 2020 and we have a plague among us sweeping around the world called the Corona Virus. Ground zero is reported to be Wuhan China. The whole world has placed itself on volunteered lock down. Here in America all schools are closed effected March fifteenth until the end of the school year. Non-essential jobs are closed. Millions are unemployed. Hundreds of thousands have died around the world. People are scared. I have been in the house for two months now. If I need to go out, I have to wear a face mask and gloves to keep myself and my family safe.

The government says the virus is caught by either touching an infected area or if an infected person cough or sneeze on you. We have been told to practice social distancing of at least six feet from another person when outside. This virus can stay on an area for up to two days.

This plague really attacks the elderly or a person with preconceived conditions. I am at a high risk because I have all the illnesses this virus likes to attack.

As of April 1st, 2020, the government has placed a self-quarantine order for thirty days. This quarantine was extended until the end of May,

2020. Easter was cancelled because no one could go outside. High school seniors' graduations were also cancelled. Everything was mailed to their homes. Day cares, bars and restaurants were also closed.

I don't know how this world is going to fix itself. All I can do is work on myself. I'm calling myself Empress Emma the head of my house and my own transformation and meditation practices.

At this last stage of my life I am the improved version of myself and I'm feeling Goddess like. 2020 has been one the worst year anyone has seen in over one hundred years. There have been more floods, droughts and tornadoes and now this virus. It's like the world is shifting or resetting to make a better place.

I don't know when we will have normalcy back in our lives. We will just have to hope for a normal summer.

I will continue to pray and meditate to the Gods. I have really gotten into sleep meditational videos now. I use sound recordings of meditating videos to tap into my subconscious mind while I'm sleeping. You Tube has a lot of these videos for your spiritual growth.

What I do is I play these soothing meditating videos while I sleep throughout the night. The selection of videos I use contain healing frequencies like the 528hz, the 432hz, and other with music for healing benefits. Your subconscious mind soaks up all the frequencies on the beats so you can heal your body while you sleep. Your body already rejuvenates it's self at night anyway, that's why you need a good eight hours of sleep every night to be fresh the next day.

I know I feel great every morning when I wake up. When I listen to the meditation videos along with a good night sleep, I really feel stress free. With this mandatory lock down and being in the house for two or more months it really has a lot of people stressed out. Not me though. I am content with staying in the house. I'm just glad I'm at a point in my life where I'm able to stay home and take care of my grandchildren while their mother has to work.

I love being the empress of the house. That's what families use to do in the past. They kept the grandmother in the house to help raise the children. Not like today generation who puts away the elderly in a nursing home. The grandchildren gets the benefit of having a loved one at home with them while the parent goes to work. Not a day care or after school program.

Chapter # 9

Third Eye Chakra

There are seven chakras used in meditation. We use chakra meditation for cleansing, clearing, balancing and healing. These chakras coincide with the organs in the body.

1. Root chakra - large intestines, rectum, and kidneys.

2. Sacral chakra - the navel, reproductive organs bladder.

3. Solar plexus - liver, gall bladder, stomach, spleen, and

small intestines.

4. Heart chakra - Heart and lungs.

5. Throat chakra- lungs and throat.

6. Third eye chakra- brain, face, nose and eyes.

7. Crown Chakra - related to whole body.

My favorite is the third eye chakra also known as " The Sixth Sense". This chakra also connects us to our intuitions, sharp sense, and the sense of observation. This chakra is governed by the 5th ray of " Concrete Knowledge". A healthy third eye gives you the power to perceive reflection from the outer world such as intuition and your sixth senses.

As I stated before I love the third eye chakra. A blocked chakra causes you to become delusional, unimaginative, and have poor memories. You tend to worry a lot when your third eye is blocked, and you have poor concentration.

You know your third eye chakra is stimulated and open when you have a tingling sensation or pressure on your brow. You may see colors, shadows, lights, auras, or even spirits. Your dreams may even become vivid and seem real.

I think I mentioned this before but one of my dreams was so real that I actually fell out of my bed because I was trying to get away from a bright light or what I thought was a being of some kind. My subconscious mind wasn't ready to face that realization in my dream at that time.

When you are in your dream state, that's a good time for your ancestors or the Gods to try and talk to you. After I fell out of my bed I just laid there for a minute trying to remember my dream. Another reason I laid there was because I was trying to contemplate how I was actually going to get up from the floor. You see, I have bad knees and it is hard for me to get up after I have fallen down. Once I finally got up off the floor, I sat on the edge of the bed. I was breathing extremely fast because my dream felt so real.

Later that year While I was on my spiritual retreat, I asked the spiritual master about my dream. He was the one who explained that the deity was trying to come to me in my dream, but I wasn't ready to face it, and that's why I fell out of the bed.

On another occasion when my sixth sense came into play was while I was watching my two-year-old grandson. I left a candle burning on my altar and I must have dosed off for a minute because the next thing I remember was It felt like someone was calling me to wake up. While I was sitting on the couch I opened my eyes to flames coming out of the chair next to the altar. For just a moment I sat there not believing my eyes. Then the flames started to burn through the chair onto the carpet. That's when I came to and jumped up, ran to the kitchen, got water in pitcher, and poured it on the flames. That wasn't enough to put out the flames. I made three more trips to the kitchen for more water. I never ran so fast. By this time the smoke alarm was going off in the hall. I was choking but I got the fire to go out.

I quickly opened all the windows

and Chris and I went into the back bedroom where we opened up the bedroom window. After the smoke cleared all the rooms, I tried to figure out how my chair caught fire.

Chris was two years old and all I could think of was he must have put something in the candle that caught fire then fell in the chair. I'm just thankful nothing worse happened.

If my subconscious mind or my guardian angel waking me up at the right time it would have been much worse. Or it could have even been my third eye chakra. The third eye chakra signals the subconscious mind. This chakra keeps you in tune with intuition and with meditation. With practice you can receive messages from the past or future.

I'm still working on this concept of receiving messages from past or future, but my subconscious mind and my intuition have helped me on many occasions. I believe that believing is the key. If you believe you can make anything happen.

Chapter # 10

Spirituality

The end is the beginning and the beginning is the end. I would like to take this time to recap about my spirituality and my rebirth.

My reincarnation will be an ongoing process until I cross over to the other realm. I'm praying at my altar every morning to my Lord Ganesha and my ancestors. I pray for protection for my family and also for the world to heal itself from the plague.

Lord Ganesha is the deity I most

relate to. Ganesha is known as the God of wisdom and success and the destroyer of all obstacles. Just as the world is resetting by bringing the virus to kill hundreds of thousands of people as history has repeated itself before.

" From the Washington Post"

Here's History's deadliest pandemics, and from ancient Rome to Modern America.

165-180 A.D

Antonine Plague

Death: 5 million

541-542 A.D

Plague of Justinia

Death:30-50 million

1347-1352

Black Death

Death: 75-200 million

1520-unknown

New World Smallpox

Death: 25-55 million

1665- Great Plague of London

Death: 75000-10000

1817-1923

The Cholera Pandemic

Death: 1 million

1918-1920

The 1918 Flu

Death: 50 million caused by H1N1

1957-1958

Asian Flu

Death: 1 million Caused by H2N2

2009

Swine Flu

Death:200,000 caused by H1N1

2020Covid-19

Total confirmed so far 3,074,948

Total; Deaths so far 213,273

Countries infected 185.

As you can see the time is now more than ever that we need to pray. Businesses and schools have been closed for over two months. Every state has been on quarantine. If you must go outside you must wear a mask and gloves. The elderly and people with illnesses are more prone to the virus.

This is a prayer I found from the past and it is more relevant today more than ever.

You who dwells in the shelter of the most high, who abides in the shadow of the omnipotent. I say to you of the Lord who is my refuge and my stronghold, my God in whom I trust, that he will save you from the destructive pestilence. He will cover you with his opinions and you will find refuge under his wings. His truth is a shield and an armor. You will not fear the terror of the night, nor the arrow that flies by the pestilence that prowls in the darkness nor the destruction that ravages at noon. A thousand may fall at your left side and ten thousand at your right but it shall not reach you. You need only see the retribution of the wicked because you have said, The Lord is my shelter and you have made the most high your heaven. No evil will be fall you. No plague will come near your tent. For he will instruct his angels in your behalf to guard you in all your ways.

I believe in this prayer and I pray it every day. I pray for blessings and protection. I pray for the world to be made whole again. I pray for my own rebirth. I pray that my reincarnation will make me a better version of myself.

Peace and Love.

This is a poem I was inspired to write called, 3rd Eye Awakening

I was never told but I always knew

I was put here for a purpose not just for you

I'm always at the helm of my destiny

See you at another time in another realm I'm Ms. Emmy

Back to the future present past this reality will never last

To all my ancestors watching over me

All I can say is Ase' and peace

While I awaken my subconscious mind

I give praises to all that's divine

I now remove this generational karma

Mama Daddy nothing else can harm us

I call out to Lord Ganesha my protector and savior

Thank You, Thank you, Thank you, three times the favor.   By Empress Emma

Resources:

Chris Enlightened

YouTube

Nu Meditation Music

Energy Healing Music Channel

The American Heritage Dictionary of the

English language, Fifth Edition

The Washington Post

Dedications:

Mama Vivian Maxwell

My son Chris Enlightened

Daughter Teenya

Grandchildren:

Devyn

Mya

Antonio

&

Christopher

I love each and every one of you with all my heart. Peace and Love

The reincarnation of Empress Emma is my reality of realizing that awakening my subconscious mind is the key to knowledge of self, life, and death.

Author Empress Emma

Made in the USA
Columbia, SC
15 May 2023

16232567R00090